Library Technology
REPORTS
Expert Guides to Library Systems and Services

Blockchain in Libraries

Michael Meth

ALA TechSource
alatechsource.org

American Library Association

Library Technology
REPORTS

ALA TechSource purchases fund advocacy, awareness, and accreditation programs for library professionals worldwide.

Volume 55, Number 8
Blockchain in Libraries
ISBN: 978-0-8389-1821-0
DOI: https://doi.org/10.5860/ltr.55n8

American Library Association
50 East Huron St.
Chicago, IL 60611-2795 USA
alatechsource.org
800-545-2433, ext. 4299
312-944-6780
312-280-5275 (fax)

Advertising Representative
Samantha Imburgia
simburgia@ala.org
312-280-3244

Editor
Samantha Imburgia
simburgia@ala.org
312-280-3244

Copy Editor
Judith Lauber

Production
ALA Production Services

Cover Design
Alejandra Diaz and ALA Production Services

Library Technology Reports (ISSN 0024-2586) is published eight times a year (January, March, April, June, July, September, October, and December) by American Library Association, 50 E. Huron St., Chicago, IL 60611. It is managed by ALA TechSource, a unit of the publishing department of ALA. Periodical postage paid at Chicago, Illinois, and at additional mailing offices. POSTMASTER: Send address changes to Library Technology Reports, 50 E. Huron St., Chicago, IL 60611.

ALA TechSource
alatechsource.org

About the Author

Michael Meth is the Associate Dean, Research and Learning Services, at the Florida State University (FSU) Libraries. Michael has the pleasure of overseeing a team dedicated to shaping the libraries' services for students and faculty, creating programs and partnerships that enhance and support research at all levels, and ensuring that the libraries are integrated into teaching and learning at FSU. Before coming to FSU, Michael was a librarian at the University of Toronto (UofT) libraries. There he was the Director of the Ontario Institute for Studies in Education (OISE) Library and also held an appointment as adjunct faculty at the Institute for Management of Innovation at UofT Mississauga. Michael has taught courses on leadership for aspiring librarians and information professionals at UofT's iSchool and a finance course in the Department of Management at UofT Mississauga. Prior to this appointment at OISE, Michael was the Director of the Li Koon Chun Finance Learning Centre at the UofT Mississauga Library. He holds a master of information studies degree from UofT's Faculty of Information Studies (now the iSchool) and a bachelor of business administration degree from the Schulich School of Business at York University. In 2014, Michael was selected as a Senior Fellow at UCLA's Graduate School of Education and Information Studies, and in 2013, he participated in Harvard's Leadership Institute for Academic Librarians.

Abstract

This issue of *Library Technology Reports* (vol. 55, no. 8), "Blockchain in Libraries," examines the application of blockchain in libraries. Blockchain technology has the ability to transform how libraries provide services and organize information. To date, most of these applications are still in the conceptual stage. However, sooner or later, development and implementation will follow. This report is intended to provide a primer on the technology and some thought starters. In chapter 2, the concept of blockchain is explained. Chapter 3 provides eight thought and conversation starters that look at how blockchain could be applied in libraries. Chapter 4 looks at the barriers and challenges of implementing blockchain in libraries. Chapter 5 raises some questions around ethical issues that librarians should consider with respect to blockchain implementation.

Subscriptions

alatechsource.org/subscribe

Contents

Chapter 1

Introduction

This issue of *Library Technology Reports* was originally proposed in 2018, when blockchain was still considered an exploratory technology. It stands to reason that in 2019, the year when this report is published, blockchain still is very much a technology with significant unexplored potential. To date, the main application of blockchain technology has been in the arena of cryptocurrency. Whether through the news, from excited computer-savvy friends, or over a family dinner, you may have heard of cryptocurrencies such as Bitcoin, Ethereum, Ripple, or many of the other thousands of coins that have been created in the last few years. Their rapid rise from speculative digital tokens (considered untraceable by regulators and with little intrinsic value) to tokens with quasi-currency status and an air of legitimacy was so fast that many considered this the twenty-first-century version of the tulip mania that swept the Netherlands in the seventeenth century.[1] The rise of Bitcoin has been well documented, starting from an obscure white paper in 2008 by the mysterious Satoshi Nakamoto to a valuation of USD$20,089 per unit at its peak in December 2017.[2] However, neither Bitcoin nor blockchain is a completely new phenomenon. Bitcoin is the first cryptocurrency that gained relatively widespread adoption, but as Narayanan and colleagues outlined, it was preceded by many other digital cryptographic currencies and by many attempts (which often failed) at distributed ledgers for digitally encrypted credit cards online in the 1990s.[3]

For various reasons, other cryptocurrencies did not gain the level of awareness and popularity that Bitcoin has reached. One of the reasons for Bitcoin's success is its ingenious use of the distributed ledger that underlies the Bitcoin blockchain (as outlined in Satoshi's white paper). Interestingly, this is where the first linkage to libraries can be made. The Bitcoin blockchain bears conceptual resemblance to distributed computing and to a concept that many in libraries are familiar with: LOCKSS. LOCKSS, which stands for Lots of Copies Keep Stuff Safe, is an initiative originally started by the Stanford Libraries in 1999. David Rosenthal, cofounder of the LOCKSS initiative, provided a history of how LOCKSS and other decentralized computing protocols are linked to our current understanding of blockchain technology on his blog.[4]

Stanford University: LOCKSS
https://www.lockss.org

Although blockchain is most commonly associated with cryptocurrencies, there is much more to this new technology than just cryptocurrency. Libraries, as organizations and as enterprises, will be impacted by this technology in numerous ways—from outside the library, where vendors will start deploying products and services based on blockchain, to libraries themselves leveraging blockchain to improve their systems and organizations. The ways in which blockchain will find its way into libraries are still uncharted. However, initiatives are under way, such as the work being done as part of an IMLS-funded grant at the iSchool at San José State University, and efforts such as this report.[5] The ideas for blockchain in libraries are still mostly at the conceptual level, and some possible use cases are presented in chapter 3. Whether these or completely different use cases will become successful implementations remains to be seen. How libraries implement blockchain will determine the impact of the technology and how it transforms the way we work with each other and our communities. This report will investigate the implications of blockchain technology for libraries from a variety of angles. First, we will introduce the ideas underlying this technology. Subsequent chapters will present thought starters for possible applications of blockchain technology in libraries, museums, and archives.[6] The report will wrap up with a discussion of barriers, challenges, and ethical considerations around the implementation of blockchain technology in our libraries. Ultimately, the goal for this report is to accessibly introduce the technology and to provide thought and conversation starters to help libraries examine this complex topic and prepare themselves for the changes ahead.

Notes

1. True crypto enthusiasts will vehemently balk at the notion that crypto tokens are currency. Much of the cryptocurrency movement was founded in order to cut out the middlemen and free the exchange of value—i.e., traditional fiat currency—from government scrutiny and regulation. Blockchain's decentralized ledger with its built-in privacy protocols presented a perfect system until it grew too large to be ignored by governments. Blockchain enthusiasts and purists consider the notion of "currency" too close to the idea of fiat currency—i.e., currency issued and managed by governments.
2. Satoshi Nakamoto, "Bitcoin: A Peer-to-Peer Electronic Cash System," white paper, Bitcoin.org, 2008, https://bitcoin.org/bitcoin.pdf; CoinMarketCap, Bitcoin Statistics, accessed September 7, 2019, https://coinmarketcap.com/currencies/bitcoin.
3. Arvind Narayanan, Joseph Bonneau, Edward Felten, Andrew Miller, and Steven Godlfeder, "Bitcoin and Cryptocurrency Technologies: A Comprehensive Introduction," draft, February 9, 2016, https://d28rh4a8wq0iu5.cloudfront.net/bitcointech/readings/princeton_bitcoin_book.pdf.
4. David Rosenthal, "Blockchain: What's Not to Like?," DSHR's Blog, December 10, 2018, https://blog.dshr.org/2018/12/blockchain-whats-not-to-like.html
5. "Blockchains for the Information Profession: A Project of the SJSU iSchool," San José State University, accessed September 8, 2019, https://ischoolblogs.sjsu.edu/blockchains.
6. In this report, I almost exclusively refer to libraries. Please note that in most cases, especially as it relates to the thought starters in chapter 3, museums and archives can often be substituted as allied terms.

Chapter 2

Blockchain Primer

Most simply put, blockchain is technology built on the concept of the distributed ledger. So, what does this actually mean? In a well-functioning blockchain, the original moment of data creation is recorded in the blockchain ledger as the original "block."[1] This transaction and each subsequent transaction after this original entry updates the ledger. The ledger is replicated on all the nodes participating in the blockchain, forming a distributed ledger. Through this distributed recording mechanism, the blockchain becomes immutable and blocks can be traced back to the original entry and every other related entry in that same lineage. An apt analogy to how blockchain works and how it can transform current technology and systems is by comparing it to genealogy and the concept of the family tree. Currently, any genealogist trying to reconstruct a family history has to rely on what is known about the family and do research to reconstruct familial links by visiting census data, property records, immigration records, and so on. This is a long and laborious process depending on the level of data the genealogist desires and is able to acquire. When that family tree has been developed, it can be compared and connected to the research of other genealogists on any of the popular genealogy sites. The family tree can then be compared to other family trees for overlaps and validation. If blockchain were used as the underlying technology, then every individual in the verified family tree could be established as one entry on the blockchain, created out of a "transaction" from two previous blocks. Thus, each record is linked to its preceding records and, by default, to every future record. Blocks within a genealogical blockchain could have data encoded to provide additional information on the individuals such as names, date and place of birth, height, eye color, agencies involved in adoption, links to genetic services, and so on. Thus, the blockchain could provide a verified record of the entire family tree at the press of a button in perpetuity.

Of course, this is an oversimplified representation of a blockchain. In the world of blockchain, this kind of diagram is called a Merkle tree. The original paper that introduced the Merkle tree was published in 1980 and established the basics of a blockchain protocol and how it could be cryptographically secured.[2] The Merkle tree logic allows for a very sophisticated and trusted algorithm to create unique identifiers for each block. This unique ID, called a "hash" in blockchain language, is a major feature in securing the blockchain and creating the immutable records that confirm the integrity of the data that is stored. The logic underlying the Merkle tree reduces the computational power required to verify the integrity of the blockchain because of the method by which hashes are created and linked to the preceding block in the blockchain. This mechanism affords participants in the blockchain a very high degree of security and privacy and has led to the Merkle tree becoming the basis of blockchain. Figure 2.1 is an example of a Merkle tree. The "uberblock" at the top represents the

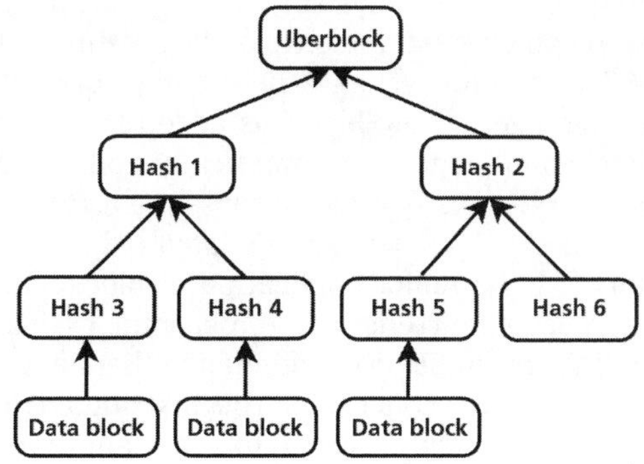

Figure 2.1
Example of a Merkle tree, a simplified representation of a blockchain structure. Source: "File:ZFS Merkle Tree 2.svg" by Markus Then is licensed under CC BY-SA 4.0 (https://creativecommons.org/licenses/by-sa/4.0/), https://commons.wikimedia.org/wiki/File:ZFS_Merkle_Tree_2.svg. Figure has been adapted; the bottom row has been updated from "Datenblock" to "Data block" and "Hash 6" has been added.

original block and each block below relates back to the original block.

However, what makes the blockchain so powerful as an application is its basis in distributed computing. In other words, the verification of the current block entry against all of its predecessors requires the availability of a network of computers that run the background checks required to validate the current record. In the most secure applications, the background checks have to be confirmed by a majority of participants in the blockchain (although a lower threshold can also be specified). The most significant benefit of this approach is that hacking the network becomes close to impossible, and even if it could be done, it would be very expensive. If one were to try to alter or forge a record, then the entire lineage of the record back to the original kernel would have to be changed, which in a distributed ledger would require knowing and hacking all of the computing nodes involved in retrieving and verifying those records. This introduces a significant degree of complexity that, although not impenetrable (in theory), does present a significant challenge that may outweigh the motivations of potential hackers. Consequently, blockchain has been considered in a wide variety of applications and scenarios where security and immutability are significant concerns.

The distributed ledger combines the technology underlying distributed computing with the concept of the ledger used in accounting. The distributed ledger is a digitized version of the paper ledger where transactions are recorded as they occur, thus providing the accounting and documentation required to ensure that transactions have taken place. In a ledger, one might record amounts, parties involved, time of transaction, and other pertinent information. The distributed ledger takes this information, places it online, and distributes identical copies of the ledger to all the computers in the system, thereby ensuring that validated copies exist in multiple places (similar to the LOCKSS principle). When a new entry (or in blockchain language, a new block) is added to the ledger, the distributed ledger is automatically updated across all nodes in the system. Every subsequent transaction is now added to this new and updated ledger.

Thus far, the major application of blockchain has been for cryptocurrency. Cryptocurrencies, such as Bitcoin, Ethereum, Ripple, and many others have been developed on the concept of the distributed ledger. They have come into existence to act as alternatives to traditional government-backed currencies such as the dollar or euro. As alternative quasi-currencies, cryptocurrencies have leveraged blockchain and enabled an entirely new global network of currency transactions. This has been done by employing blockchain as a distributed database working on computers located all over the world. These computers work on a system of randomly assigned verifications needed to maintain the integrity of the blockchain. Computers participating in this verification process are called “miners.” They engage in calculations of varying intensity and difficulty that work on solving the unique codes used in every block. This unique code or hash is a cryptographically-secured string of numbers. As an incentive for participating in this process, at certain intervals, miners are issued a reward. Typically, miners receive a unit of value of the blockchain’s currency seeking validation (e.g., one Bitcoin). This process is important, as we will explore later, since there has to be incentive in the system to ensure that enough computers are participating in the verification, which in turn ensures the security and speed of the blockchain. To put this incentive into perspective, one Bitcoin at its peak value in 2017 was worth over $20,000. Although the price of Bitcoin fluctuates significantly and in 2019 Bitcoin has been trading in a range from the low $3,000s to just over $13,000, the incentive often outweighs the costs of time and energy expended in the process of mining.[3] To further explain the principle behind how Bitcoins are awarded, imagine 100 miners are working on the calculation tasks required to verify the blockchain. The blockchain may have been set up to award a token after every 1,000th verification is completed. If miner 1 solves verification number 999, it would get nothing. If miner 2 solves verification number 1,000, it would receive one Bitcoin. If miner 3 solves verification number 1,001, it would get nothing, and so on, until somebody solves verification number 2,000. Thus the process provides both incentive and motivation, but also a sufficient amount of randomness so that all are engaged to the best of their abilities. In libraries, the financially motivated incentive mechanisms of cryptocurrency do not exist. However, other incentives may have to be developed. Depending on the applications, consortial agreements may predetermine contributions from those participating in the blockchain. For example, suppose thirty libraries decide to develop a blockchain and contractually dedicate a certain amount of computing power to allow for the blockchain to always be available and up to date. In that case, the contract is in place; other incentives are not needed. However, larger public blockchain applications would need new incentive models that would appeal to those required to participate. What exactly those will be will depend on the application and who is expected or required to participate.

Private versus Public Blockchains

Blockchains have two main variations that have significant impact and influence over how they function, who can participate, and who has control over them. A blockchain can be private or public.[4] Private blockchains are, as suggested by the name, exclusive in nature. Only those invited and authorized can participate in a private blockchain. This creates a controlled environment with a limited number of authorized participants. Public blockchains are exactly the opposite. They are open networks that anyone can participate in, adding and verifying transactions. Unlike private blockchains, public blockchains are typically decentralized. The network protects itself through scale and enabling any member of the blockchain to audit and validate the data. Typically, this kind of blockchain is involved when discussing cryptocurrency applications. Conversely, in a private blockchain, the distributed network is limited, and all users are known. Whether a blockchain is private or public is up to the developer of the application. This has to be determined at the very beginning stages. In libraries, we may find that both types of blockchains have applications and can be employed depending on the problem at hand. The thought starters provided in the next chapter will address the benefits and challenges associated with these two types of blockchains and will present use cases that consider the benefits of private versus public blockchains.

Power Consumption and Computing Power

Public blockchains are designed to provide immutable records of transactions. The underlying value of a public blockchain is derived from trust established by the decentralized system ensuring that single actors and coordinated schemes to subvert it will be unsuccessful. The blockchain is available to all and can be verified by any member. For future transactions to be validated, a majority of members need to verify the blockchain, also known as "proof of work." This process of verification is complex and needs to happen quickly in order for the blockchain to function efficiently. As the blockchain grows and transactions increase, the level of complexity grows, which leads to increased need for computing power. As a result, the increasing demands on computers and processors to continuously verify the blockchain lead to massive energy consumption. Various large blockchain applications have been estimated to consume more electricity than entire nations over comparable periods of time.[5] However, this issue will not typically arise in the way most libraries would employ blockchain technology. If a library were to deploy a public blockchain, then the transaction volume would not be even close to the transactions required by cryptocurrencies such as Bitcoin or Ethereum. The reason for this discrepancy is in the frequency and in the increments with which cryptocurrencies trade. Cryptocurrencies can trade in fractions to the eighth decimal (i.e., 0.00000001 Bitcoin). Thus, a Bitcoin can be divided and subdivided and recombined over and over. This complexity, combined with the frequency at which currencies can be exchanged, is far in excess of any transactions that are likely to occur in libraries, such as circulation data or patron data. (Such transactions also by their nature are unlikely to be divided down to the eighth decimal.) Furthermore, the "proof of work" requirement could be set at a different and lower rate from what is required in cryptocurrency applications, thus significantly reducing the need for computing power. In a private blockchain, the permissions for those who participate can be set very differently from a public blockchain—so differently in fact that power consumption could be much better managed because the private blockchain with all participants known would be a trusted and reliable recording mechanism. Proofs or verifications might not be required, and certainly not in the same way that a public blockchain would require. Furthermore, a private blockchain would serve well in many library applications since it would allow for faster verification. It would not need the 51 percent proof of work consensus mechanism required to prevent fraudulent activity in many public blockchains due to the anonymity of the users and miners. There are many versions of private blockchains emerging, and they are being branded in a number of ways. For example, Hyperledger was developed by the Linux Foundation in 2016 and has found significant support from many commercial entities across the spectrum of consulting, banking, and manufacturing industries.

Hyperledger
https://www.hyperledger.org

What Can Be Encoded in a Block?

Blocks on the blockchain are information containers. They can hold a wide variety of content. At the very least, a block stores its own unique identifier, or "hash," that links it to all blocks preceding it and all subsequent blocks. Each block is uniquely identified through its hash, which is automatically generated and ensures there is no ambiguity between different blocks. However, much more can be stored in a block. In addition to this identifier information, blocks can store data of all kinds related to a transaction, such as the following:

- time
- date
- measurements (e.g., height, width, weight, etc.)
- text

- transactional information
- computer code that can trigger actions (usually referred to as "smart contracts")

These various kinds of data can be automatically generated or can be manually added. In practice, the data stored is readable across blocks. The data in the blocks can then be queried and analyzed. The size of what can be encoded in a block is limited only by the specifications set by the creator of the blockchain. The blocks can be small and allow only a few kilobytes of data, or they can be quite large and allow several megabytes of data. As the technology evolves, it will be possible to attach PDF and image files, audio files, video files, and files of other formats that have not been previously associated with blockchain. One limitation thus far has been related to the computing power required to process building, storing, and verifying blocks. Since every block includes information linked to previous blocks, there has been some concern about the overall size of the blockchain database. As technology advances and computing power increases, the boundaries of these limitations will be tested and will expand. It remains to be seen whether Moore's Law,[6] the increasing speed of the internet (some will remember the early days of the public internet and dial-up modems), or the evolution of the cell phone to the current smartphone is an apt analogy. However, as with all successful technologies, increasing adoption will lead to increasing investment, and ingenuity in how the technology can be optimized and improved will follow.

Blockchain and Privacy

One of the keys to blockchain technology that has made it viable for cryptocurrencies is the privacy features. These features constitute a key component of the blockchain and could be considered built in by design. There are three main areas in which the blockchain is particularly strong:

- public and private keys
- the public blockchain
- the private blockchain

Public and Private Keys

Participants in a blockchain have to gain access to it. In order to do so, a participant has to register or be issued a private key. Depending on the blockchain rules, the participant's public key can be issued by the owner of the blockchain, or the participant can autogenerate a key, which ensures even greater privacy. The public key is a complex alphanumeric sequence that is unique to the participant. However, participants in the blockchain are not limited to only one private key and thus can have multiple accounts. A complex algorithm converts private keys to public keys. Public keys are used for the record-keeping of the blockchain. The algorithm used to derive public keys from private keys cannot be reverse engineered, which ensures that the private key always remains private. In the blockchain, when a transaction is initiated, the public key is recorded with the blocks to provide accountability of the transacting party. The public address can be queried, and transactions can be traced back to the public key. Because public keys cannot be reverse engineered to the private key, owners of a private key remain anonymous unless they reveal their private keys. Due to this extreme privacy function, private keys cannot be recovered once lost. It is worth noting that the data that has been encoded in the blockchain remains there forever due to the immutability of the blockchain. There are countless stories in cryptocurrency of lost private keys, which means that the coins associated with those keys cannot be recovered by the original owner and thus are lost forever. This is akin to losing the keys to a treasure chest that has been hidden somewhere. In other words, the contents of the treasure chest still exist, as does the record of their existence. However, the contents have now become irretrievably lost. As it happens, many private keys have been lost. Estimates point to roughly 17 to 23 percent of all Bitcoins ever mined having been lost.[7] This can prove to be a challenge if a user were to lose their private key. However, this tradeoff in convenience has to be accepted if this level of privacy is desired. Unlike with a password to an email account, where a forgotten password can be retrieved by answering a few security questions to access the account again, a forgotten private key is irretrievably lost and the account is no longer accessible.

Public Blockchain

In a public blockchain, everybody can join. Using a private key, that has been converted to a public key allows anybody with an internet connection and a computing device able to run the blockchain software to participate. Since the public blockchain is a distributed ledger of all transactions, no single user can corrupt the data. When a transaction takes place on the blockchain, a new block is created. However, the block does not get added to the blockchain until it has been verified by a majority of the participants. Depending on the number of participants and a few other factors, this verification can take place in real time or may take a longer amount of time. Most importantly, though, the consensus required to verify the blockchain ensures that the security, privacy, and integrity of the blockchain are maintained.

Private Blockchain

In a private blockchain, the owner of the blockchain has significant influence over its design and subsequent operations. As a result, a private blockchain is a less secure and private type of blockchain. Here, the participants in the blockchain are known, and blocks can be altered at the owner's discretion. While this may pose a privacy challenge, it does not mean that the blockchain cannot be maintained with strict privacy controls in place. Therefore, depending on the desired application, a private blockchain could be a viable application that ensures security.

How Do Blocks Talk to Each Other?

The blocks in a blockchain talk to each other by being linked in a very linear way. The Merkle tree diagram (see figure 2.1) provides a visual representation of how each block is linked back to the preceding block. In blockchain, the hash from the first block is combined with the hash from the second block to make a new, unique combination. The next block combines the earlier block and the new information by adding its unique signature. The hash itself is an encrypted and complex alphanumeric combination, ensuring that the combination is unique. Here is a very simplistic way to think of the way hashes work:

Original hash: A1
Next block hash: A1 + new hash, i.e., A2 → new block hash of A1A2
Next block hash: A1A2 + new hash, i.e., A3 → new block hash of A2A3
And so on . . .

Through this combination of hashes, the entire blockchain can be verified and traced back to the original block. The ingenuity of this method is that while one can always trace known hashes backward, one cannot predict future hashes. If A1A2 is known, then hackers could go back and try to alter A1. However, they would have to alter all the preceding blocks in the blockchain. If A2A3 has already been created, the blockchain would detect the fraud attempt. More importantly, since the blockchain lives in the cloud and is replicated on many computers, there will always be copies of the original blockchain available to verify against. In cryptocurrency, where this kind of attack would be a grave concern, the developer community has decided on a concept called "proof of work." Proof of work requires 51 percent of the network to confirm the transaction, thereby making a coordinated attack on the blockchain nearly impossible. This built-in security ensures, as the blockchain community refers to it, immutability—that is, that the block cannot be altered after it has been created, verified and added to the blockchain.

Problem or Solution: Which One Came First?

In libraries we deal with myriad challenges on a regular basis. We try to create engaging environments. We try to work within our budgets. We work with our patrons, users, scholars, students, clients, or whatever other user-specific term is employed in your organization. We work with each other across divisions, different locations, consortia, and so on. We try to measure and share the value we add to our environments. All of these challenges are looking for solutions. However, as the old aphorism reminds us, "If your only tool is a hammer, all problems look like nails." Thus the question arises, "What problems are we able to solve with blockchain?" Throughout this report, we will think through the "why" and "so what" related to blockchain as a solution to the problems and opportunities presented. For what it is worth, libraries function, and function well at that. We share catalogs and records. We have patron records in our databases. We manage our collection budgets. We issue library cards. And, to say the very least, we are keenly aware of issues related to privacy. The author of this report posits that some of these areas could be significantly improved by employing blockchain as a technology. However, even though blockchain technology can address these issues and concerns, often the implementation will raise new issues. Ultimately, each case will have its own specific context that will decide whether the technology is transformative and of sufficient value for consideration and implementation in your organization. In chapter 3, we will present thought starters so that you, the reader, may consider the various opportunities and challenges to make your own determination about whether blockchain is an appropriate solution to your problems and whether it meets the ethical standards you hold yourself to.

Why Should Libraries Care about Blockchain?

So what? We have now established some of the basics of blockchain, but why should libraries care? Libraries should care because blockchain is here to stay. Many corporations have bought into the idea of blockchain to support their enterprises. As acceptance grows and use cases emerge, our library community will be presented with applications based on blockchain technology. It is not farfetched to think that library systems will be developed leveraging blockchain. Perhaps our next-generation integrated library systems will be built on open standards and blockchain will be used to secure user records in the system. Thus, it behooves us as libraries to be informed and at least conversant on the topic of blockchain so that we can truly evaluate whether we are being presented with feasible applications and systems or just alluring trends and marketing pitches. Applications that we have not thought of yet will be developed that leverage blockchain. Therefore, we have a significant opportunity to contribute to the development of blockchain technology within libraries, museums, and archives. Some opportunities for the use of blockchain will be related to the scholarly record, research, funding mechanisms, and so on. Thus, it would be wise for libraries to prepare for these conversations. Another likely important connection will be linking blockchain with the emerging technologies of big data and artificial intelligence. However, perhaps the best answer to why libraries should care about blockchain is because the technology provides us with the possibility to develop significantly improved systems as compared to where we are today.

In the thought starters in the next chapter, we will explore some of these concepts and provide more details on how blockchain may be employed in various libraries-related scenarios.

Notes

1. For a fascinating account of how a cryptocurrency was launched, you can access Molly Webster, reporter, "The Ceremony," podcast, produced by Matt Kielty and Molly Webster, Radiolab, WNYC Studios, July 14, 2017, https://www.wnycstudios.org/story/ceremony.
2. Ralph C. Merkle, "Protocols for Public Key Cryptosystems," in *Proceedings of the 1980 IEEE Symposium on Security and Privacy, Oakland, California, USA, April 14–16, 1980* (Silver Spring, MD: IEEE Computer Society Press, 1980), 122–34, http://www.merkle.com/papers/Protocols.pdf.
3. CoinMarketCap, Bitcoin statistics, accessed September 7, 2019, https://coinmarketcap.com/currencies/bitcoin.
4. Demiro Massessi, "Public vs. Private Blockchain in a Nutshell," Medium, December 12, 2018, https://medium.com/coinmonks/public-vs-private-blockchain-in-a-nutshell-c9fe284fa39f.
5. Garrick Hileman and Michel Rauchs, "2017 Global Cryptocurrency Benchmarking Study," April 6, 2017, last revised September 20, 2017, https://papers.ssrn.com/sol3/papers.cfm?abstract_id=2965436; Jingming Li, Nianping Li, Jinqing Peng, Haijiao Cui, and Zhibin Wu, "Energy Consumption of Cryptocurrency Mining: A Study of Electricity Consumption in Mining Cryptocurrencies," *Energy* 168 (2019): 160–68, https://doi.org/10.1016/j.energy.2018.11.046.
6. "Moore's Law 40th Anniversary Press Kit," Intel, accessed September 7, 2019, https://www.intel.com/pressroom/kits/events/moores_law_40th/index.htm.
7. Louise Matsakis, "How WIRED Lost $100,000 in Bitcoin," *Wired*, May 28, 2018, https://www.wired.com/story/wired-lost-bitcoin; for an open source download on Bitcoin blockchain analysis, see Harry Kalodner, "BlockSci: A Platform for Blockchain Science and Exploration," Freedom to Tinker, Center for Information Technology Policy, Princeton University, September 11, 2017, https://freedom-to-tinker.com/2017/09/11/blocksci-a-platform-for-blockchain-science-and-exploration.

Chapter 3

Case Studies and Thought Starters

This chapter will present eight case studies. These case studies will explore the current environment and how blockchain may be employed. However, at the time of publication, to the best of our knowledge, none of these blockchain applications have been implemented. In other words, it might be advisable to think of these case studies as thought starters. Interested readers may want to employ them to educate themselves or perhaps to explore the feasibility of these ideas. So, proceed with caution and enjoy the exploration.

1. Library Acquisitions

Libraries manage significant amounts of money through our budgets, and one of the most substantial budget lines is in acquisitions. The complex process of library acquisitions is well documented, leading from product development by a vendor to library subscription or purchase to the eventual sunsetting of the product or subscription. This process can span several decades or take place rather quickly. So how might blockchain be applied? One scenario would be to employ it for contract management related to the content covered by the contract. This works particularly well in scenarios where content is delivered digitally. Traditionally, a library finds out about a content collection that a vendor has developed. The library evaluates the product, enters negotiations with the vendor, and agrees to a price, and then that collection becomes accessible. A few years pass, the collection is in use, and the contract gets renewed following a new negotiation. As part of the new contract, new items may be added to the collection, old ones may be removed, and access may be renegotiated from single user to unlimited users. Over time, libraries create many of these contracts and systems. In an ideal situation, these contracts are well documented, accessible, and properly enforced. In real life, several points of failure can occur. Contracts are signed and subsequently lost, perhaps even just kept in a well-meaning signer's inbox. Agreements specify rules and limitations for the content. However, the systems used by libraries may or may not be able to comply with the rules.

If vendor contracts could be encoded in a blockchain, then with the right permissions in place to protect privacy and confidentiality, there would then be a permanent unalterable record of the original. Smart contracts in the blockchain could be established to facilitate access to the materials and provide updates. Whether a library buys access to 100 e-books or 10,000 journal articles, smart contracts embedded in the blockchain could facilitate the execution and access to the content. In other words, perfect compliance with the contract would be guaranteed to the library and the vendor. Since blockchain is incredibly scalable, expanding the number of titles or articles mediated by the blockchain would not pose a challenge. So if an original contract specifies a small number of items and a subsequent contract specifies a greater number, entries could be batch loaded into the blockchain. In the scenario of a shrinking contract, a batch action could also update the availability of content. If access rules change (e.g., from a one-user license to an unlimited-concurrent license), then a batch upload to the blockchain could update the smart contracts in the block to instantly update the accessibility.

Another benefit of blockchain would be the possibility of using cryptocurrencies for payment. If a library and a vendor transact in the same currency, the benefits would be limited (e.g., a purchase in US dollars from a US-based institution). However, often libraries work across boundaries—for example, a Canadian library buying content from a US vendor, a European library buying content from an Asian vendor, and so on. In those scenarios, contracts are subject to fluctuations in the exchange rate between the currencies of the countries. In a low volatility environment, this poses no risk, but in environments where exchange rates can vary significantly over time, this can pose significant problems. For example, if the US dollar rises by 20 percent over three years in relation to the Canadian dollar, then the cost of the contract to a Canadian library buying from a US vendor would rise by 20 percent. Furthermore, there are often charges for the exchange of currency, which also increases the cost of the transaction. These kinds of fluctuations and fees are difficult to absorb in library budgets. If cryptocurrency were to be used, then there would be no exchange fees as no exchange of currency would take place. The only possible complication would be fluctuation in the exchange rate between the countries' currencies and the cryptocurrency.

For various reasons, blockchain would make a lot of sense in an acquisitions scenario. How strongly a library or vendor feels about the need to remain in compliance with the rules specified by the contract would determine whether blockchain would work well. Because this scenario is limited to verification between the vendor, the library, and the users of the content, a private blockchain would be feasible here. Making that decision would limit the processing and computing required, which would also limit the cost associated with power consumption. Typically, usage for licensed content is limited. Much of the content that is licensed is used seldom, but it needs to be available and discoverable. The blockchain could help with facilitating this access and discoverability. However, due to the low volume of transactions expected and who the stakeholders are, most of the computing could be handled in-house via a private blockchain.

A library would have to implement the blockchain for contract management. The system would have to be able to handle multiple vendors and enable blocks to be programmed to handle the rules set out in every contract. The library would then have to develop a compatible authentication system to allow its users to authenticate and discover content. The vendors would then have to collaborate on developing an authentication method that matches the verification provided from the blockchain for access to the content requested. There are many obvious benefits to a system like this, as opposed to many libraries' use of spreadsheets and inbox searches. If libraries were adroit at creating and maintaining these records through relational databases where all of these contracts, access parameters, and vendor relationships could live, then there might not be a need for a blockchain. However, that is not usually the case, and we have to consider ways to make this process easier and more consistent, almost from scratch.

2. Collections Maintenance

Libraries own and subscribe to many materials. Typically, the materials we have access to, whether owned or leased, are stored in a catalog of some kind. The catalog is typically provided by a third-party vendor, which sells it as an integrated library system (ILS) or library management system (LMS). Depending on the type of ILS, the size and complexity of holdings, and other factors, access to the collection can be reliable or not. Holdings data may or may not be complete. We often ask questions in libraries related to collections. Questions may be at the macro level: How many items do we have in our collections? They may be at the item level: When was this book processed? When was it purchased, and for what price? Questions may also be cross-institutional: Can we compare our holdings to those of other institutions? Lastly, we may also ask questions related to usage: How many times was this item borrowed? How many items in our collection have been accessed more than twice?

Blockchain would allow every item in our collections to be individually tracked. A block created for every holding would include data about the original acquisition, the item itself (either in MARC, RDA, or a new metadata schema), and transactions. Every time an activity takes place, the event would create a new block in the blockchain for that holding. For example, an item is borrowed. A new block would be added to the blockchain. At a minimum, this block would contain data on the item borrowed and the public key of the borrower. Unlike in current use cases, where libraries often struggle with how to treat this user data, in blockchain we would not be able to trace back to the private key. So, while the public key can be queried by those authorized to look up information on public keys, the privacy of the borrower is preserved. Employing the blockchain would allow for rapid queries and analytics. Furthermore, a well-designed blockchain could replace the ILS/LMS providers as "middlemen," and libraries could (finally) design their own tools to take care of our systems needs. A blockchain could be established at the individual library level or within counties or universities. However, a global public blockchain for all libraries would be ideal.[1] In that scenario, every library would enter its holdings. That way, collection and holdings data could easily be analyzed across any institution or organization in the world. Besides the local impact, implementing blockchain this way could also have a significant impact on interlibrary loan (ILL). Here items could be identified much more quickly and the process of lending and borrowing in ILL could be automated through smart contracts with lending institutions. Libraries could automate the process of verifying partners, keeping track of net borrowing versus net lending, and send materials. As in other scenarios, the privacy-by-design features of blockchain would serve well here.

Blockchain most certainly makes sense for this purpose. However, the scale of implementation required to make this scenario work seems daunting. A global public blockchain could address issues of interoperability between different blockchains. Blockchain as a technology is a conceptual setup influenced by different design decisions at every step of implementation, which can influence how different branches of the blockchain operate and talk to each other. A smaller implementation at a state or provincial level would also be feasible, and a likely step in a larger process, but ultimately the greatest benefit would come from a global network. That way all the world's library holdings could be documented, analyzed, verified, and tracked. This would be a great feature in cases where collections get damaged, stolen, or destroyed.

Implementation in this case would be fairly straightforward, as we could simply transfer existing record-keeping mechanisms to the blockchain. Just as with MARC or RDA, we have established protocols for cataloging and recording bibliographic collections. The major challenges would be related to the migration of existing records to the blockchain and the immense collaborations required to be successful. However, if a tool could be developed to batch upload records, this could be a frictionless transition for most libraries, which could yield significant benefits. Once the blockchain had been implemented, then libraries could either connect with third-party off-the-shelf interfaces or could develop their own customized applications. Privacy concerns around how these records would interact with the blockchain would be addressed through the blockchain's built-in privacy mechanisms. As in cryptocurrency transactions, it would be virtually impossible to trace the transactions back to the individual unless the owner of the private key elects to make their key known. Blockchain accomplishes this via the use of public and private keys that each user has. One analogy is of a one-way road by which the private key generates a public key to verify the original transaction, but the public key cannot be turned back and be connected to the private key. Thus, any analytics or tracking of the material cannot be traced back to an individual. However, analytics at the item level could be recorded and analyzed.

3. Special Collections and Archives

Special collections and archives possess rare and distinct materials. This makes their collections unique to the overall collection development process that the information profession usually engages in. These materials have been acquired under various circumstances that may or may not be documented. If purchase or donor agreements exist, they may or may not be easily available. This can lead to confusion. At what price was a collection acquired? Who was in charge of the acquisition? A collection has been donated, but what was the donor agreement? Can the collection be divided up, or must it be kept intact? How and where can it be displayed? Furthermore, proving the provenance of these materials can also be a challenge. What is the history? How has the history been verified?

In the case of archival materials, what are the retention rules? Who has access to the materials?

How are these special collections and archival materials discoverable? How are they made accessible, and to whom?

Blockchain could address the majority of these concerns. For example, if a library acquires an important historical artifact, then the library could encode the transaction and the contract in the blockchain. Additional data related to the purchase, such as cost, time, and date, can be noted. From there, the material can be made accessible through the same discovery mechanisms used in regular collection development. Alternatively, special interfaces could be developed, for example to link blockchain and discovery mechanisms. When questions arise about where or how the materials were acquired, the blockchain records attached to each item would be able to answer these questions. In worst-case scenarios, such as theft or damage, the item can be traced through the blockchain to its rightful owner. For example, if a rare book is stolen and the thief tries to sell it, then any potential buyer could verify whether the item is as described and whether it is legally for sale. This process is currently being employed in art auctions. On November 13, 2018, Christie's auction house raised over $317 million when the Barney A. Ebsworth collection was auctioned. The sale was recorded in a blockchain platform provided by Artory, a company specialized in the art market.[2] The process employed in the registry is very similar to the process special collections and archives could use. An event related to an item takes place—for example, a donation to an institution or a valuation. This triggers the creation of a new block in the registry where the original items have been recorded. The new block is added to the ledger related to the item and is now part of the blockchain. Because it is part of the blockchain, the item is now discoverable, and all events related to it are traceable.

As the Christie's example and the Artory platform show, blockchain could be a transformative technological innovation for special collections all over the world. As collections are acquired and developed, much data is accumulated. Agreements accompanying the collections, appraisals, historical documentation of the artifacts, and other materials could all be tracked and maintained in the blockchain. Through a centralized registry, collections would become more discoverable. Once collections are discoverable, the metadata would become searchable and new opportunities for scholarship and research would open up.

4. Scholarly Record

Blockchain technology can have a significant impact on the scholarly record. In a very simplified model, for example, a scholar could establish an idea in the blockchain. This would provide a record of when the idea was first established. Then, as the idea leads to written drafts, progress on research and other impacts of the research can be tracked by creating records in the blockchain. As a project reaches milestones, including publications and patents, these can be tracked in the blockchain and linked to ISBNs or DOIs. Connections with tracking services such as ORCID and OSF can also be made. Thus, the scholarly output can be linked and analyzed, allowing scholars to get credit for their work. In addition, if a blockchain-based system is established, further analysis can be conducted across topics, authors, disciplines, publishing outlets, and any media that may be used. This could revolutionize the way scholarly output is measured and analyzed, leading to whole new ways of measuring impact.

At the level of output, blockchain could also be utilized by authors to create and manage copyright licensing that extends beyond the traditional publisher model. Access to content can be managed through smart contracts that could be embedded in the blockchain for a particular scholar, article, journal, or publisher. For example, an article gets published in a traditional journal; the journal allows the self-archiving of the prepublication version of the article in the author's institutional repository. Then, the author chooses to archive a copy and wants to mediate access via a Creative Commons license. The article is now freely accessible through the repository. Any download of the article could be noted in the blockchain. If the article is cited or otherwise used in advancing other research or publications, then that interaction could also be linked in the blockchain. The primary investigator of the original research now receives credit, and the impact of the research could be measured in new and unambiguous ways. On the matter of receiving credit for research, the recording of ideas is similar to a patent registry. Those first to develop an idea and submit it receive the credit for the original idea. If an idea registry is created, disputes about first ideas could be easily resolved. However, on a more positive note, a searchable and discoverable registry of ideas could lead to new collaborations and initiatives. Since ideas precede research and publications, early indicators of new discoveries could also be created, thus pointing to new areas of discovery and reducing lag in the publication cycle.

The establishment of this system would not be complicated; however, the larger benefit could be achieved when the network's effects kick in. The larger the system gets and the more users that participate, then the larger the system's impact is. If it could be established as a standard similar to how the patent office works and if funding agencies and institutions would buy into its adoption, it could accelerate, and the benefits could be realized sooner. Perhaps the critical question is who would establish this system. Would the system be developed by academic institutions or by funding agencies? In either situation, what would be the scope of the system? Would there be regional limitations or disciplinary focus areas? Those decisions would have a significant impact on how this system would work. Some of these impacts are considered in chapter 5 of this report.

5. Analytics in the Library

The business of libraries has become increasingly complex. The days of set budgets funded on a recurring basis are long gone. Today's libraries exist in a world where the need for advocacy has become the norm. Libraries have to meet performance metrics and deliver statistics in order to provide evidence for the value they add. However, library analytics and assessment are still a challenge. The evidence and metrics we collect in our field are limited, often focused on counting physical items and simple measures such as circulation data and gate counts. However, there is much more data to be collected in libraries. From the get-go, variation in knowledge of research methods and quality control of assessment surveys or designs makes the quality of data in libraries vary significantly. Data that connects the services libraries offer with the value we add is often difficult to collect and remains limited. Using blockchain, we could start collecting data that measures interactions with services and link it with data from other parts of the organization and community. In addition, the data collected by libraries is stored in a variety of places, often linked with sensitive data or not conforming with privacy standards, which can pose all kinds of problems. This combination of data repositories includes paper records in filing cabinets and spreadsheets on laptops, computers, shared servers, personal hard drives, USB keys, and cloud-based services. Some of our storage solutions are owned by individuals, some are owned by our institutions, and some are owned by third-party providers. To be fair, much of the data collected by libraries does not require protection, high degrees of security, or access controls around it. On the other hand, frequently the tools we have available are inadequate for protecting the data that needs to be protected. As a consequence, we often have shied away from collecting data that could aid us in providing better services to our clients and partners.

Blockchain could help with analytics in the library by providing the database infrastructure that would allow data to be collected, stored, and made accessible to authorized participants. Through smart contracts, permission could be granted and only trusted members could access selected data, while other data could be made available more broadly. Examples of data that would need to be protected include individual user data, demographic information, and other sensitive information. Data requiring less protection could be related to general collections statistics or user data at an aggregate level. Through blockchain, the data that has been collected could be secured and hosted in a way where only those with the right permissions get access. The data could be accessed through APIs or other interfaces that allow for different display and analysis options. Hosting the data via blockchain also accomplishes another goal. Rather than having multiple places where data is stored with the very real possibility of losing track of data sets, the blockchain could create a singular point of access. As a result, data inventories could be completed at the press of a button, compliance requests would become quickly accessible, and data discovery would be significantly improved.

Blockchain could also be used to empower the subjects of data collection. An example would be a student who early in their academic career participated in a survey. Subsequently the student participated in many more surveys and other ways with the library—perhaps coming to a tutoring service, borrowing laptops, and so on. If the student's participation in these activities is linked to the blockchain data via their public key, the student could review years later which data has been collected and could make informed decisions using their own data. Since libraries and our institutions are increasingly moving into new areas of data analytics, this kind of user control could be innovative and very high impact.

6. Reward Programs

As we discussed in chapter 2, incentivizing distributed computing is integral to the maintenance and success of cryptocurrency blockchains. With this in mind, libraries could create tokens based on blockchain technology. A token could be set up to measure engagement with the library and library services. In theory, the token could also be expanded to take into account interactions with services beyond the library. For example, a public library could set up a token for its community, or an academic library could set one up for the campus, university, or college. In the academic scenario, students could earn tokens for attending events or workshops hosted by the library. They could earn rewards for borrowing equipment, participating in efforts to improve the library, and so on. As student earn these credits, they could exchange them for rewards, be inducted into an academic society, or be invited to special events. In this sense, the token would mimic the model set by the cryptocurrency community, where these rewards can serve as incentives and nudges to encourage participation.

Blockchain is an effective way to track data records or interactions with library services and collections. Blockchain allows analytics to be performed on transaction data, for example: How many people participated in this workshop? How many times was equipment borrowed by undergraduate students?

Here the question of privacy will probably be a primary concern for many librarians. The short answer provided by proponents of the technology is that blockchain provides the ability to track these interactions on an anonymous basis. Privacy is built into the blockchain by default. In fact, blockchain allows users to control their data to a much greater extent than anything we can offer right now. An example would be a student who enters university and during the library orientation agrees to be interviewed on video and signs a waiver. During a later visit, the student is asked to participate in a survey, which has another waiver attached. On subsequent visits to the library, the student attends a workshop and uses the tutoring service. The student also visits the library every Tuesday after class, and the library tracks the visit data from card swipes on entry and exit. In the course of all of these interactions, the student generates a lot of data. Nearing graduation, the student sees the video agreed to during the first year but doesn't recall giving permission for the video to be used. The student can now enter their profile stored on the blockchain and review the agreement. The student can decide to revoke that permission. The student then realizes that over several years of coming to the library, lots of data has been collected, and is curious about how and when this data was used. The blockchain would allow the student to query in which research studies their data was used. The student might even be able to review decisions that were made based on the data to which they contributed. Blockchain in effect allows the student to own their data and to allow or disallow usage of the data captured.

From the library's perspective, the data and agreements generated provide a safeguard for the institution as well as the ability to perform analytics. We can query without having to worry about violating user privacy because, as explained earlier, privacy is a foundational feature of the blockchain.

7. A Unified/Verified Library "Card"

Libraries interact with patrons or users usually via user accounts that are verified using an issued unique user ID and a library card. This card allows patrons to interact with the library's system and services. They can borrow materials online and in person. They can authenticate themselves online and gain access to databases or materials. This system works well and has worked well for many years. However, improvements can be accomplished via blockchain.

One major area where blockchain could improve the borrowing experience is through its privacy applications. The ALA *Library Bill of Rights* emphasizes "the right to privacy and confidentiality in their library use."[3] Currently, a patron's borrowing history is stored on servers and in library information management systems. These systems may be very sophisticated and may be set up to delete borrowing histories on some regular interval after a loan has been completed. However, there are weak points in this system. The user data is gathered when a borrowing transaction happens and is then available for some time after the transaction has concluded. We say "some time" to be purposely vague because these retention timeframes are not usually made explicit and vary from system to system. The data may be stored on a library's or a third-party server, which may be hackable, can be subpoenaed, and is more than likely backed up in more places than the average librarian or user realizes. Borrowers may benefit from accessing their borrowing data. However, once it has been deleted, we have made it inaccessible to them and to ourselves. Through the use of private and public keys, we could develop a system that would allow borrowing to take place but for the borrower's identity to be protected. Moreover, the data would be stored with the users' public keys, which they could use to access their own history and review their own data.

Another benefit of blockchain would be creating a verified system of library users that could allow users from different borrowing systems to enjoy benefits in other systems. A borrower from one state who travels to another may be able to access services immediately and without a local library card. In an academic library setting, a borrower from one institution could travel to another institution and be automatically authenticated in that library's system.

8. Blockchain for Information Literacy

Libraries are an important part in digital and information literacy education. Blockchain can be utilized to create systems to verify information. A blockchain-based system could be created that allows news articles to be uploaded, time-stamped, and verified. A reader who wants to access the material can confirm via the blockchain that the content is unaltered from the original. The article can be protected from being altered, and the distribution of fake articles could be prevented. The same goes for video and audio content. The creation of deepfake videos, where videos include seamless, digitally created content, could also be made significantly more difficult. The creator of an original video can establish via blockchain the original video. Suppose that later, a modified deepfake version were created of this original content and entered the mainstream. Using the blockchain, the video could be verified against the content that has been uploaded in the blockchain and exposed as a fake.

From a user perspective, authentication to read original material could be managed through the use of the private and public key framework. Users concerned about censorship or confidentiality could use their private key and a privacy browser to create a public key to access information that otherwise may be inaccessible to them. While metadata such as IP-based location could still be tracked, the authentication to the individual user would be obscured and privacy would be ensured.

One interesting approach to this challenge is the News Provenance Project, which is supported by the *New York Times*.[4] The project is in its infancy but is looking to address the issue of fake news via metadata that is encoded in blockchain. The challenge with this system is the massive amounts of news and the rapidity with which news is being created, which pose a challenge when it comes to keeping the network current. Many other systems are being explored and developed to address the issue of fake news, and it remains to be seen if any of them will succeed.

Moving Forward

These eight case studies are brief thought starters to introduce possible applications of blockchain in libraries. Any of the concepts can be extended to special collections, archives, museums, or other memory institutions. More importantly though, the big questions that need to be answered in all of the use cases or any others that will emerge are (*a*) whether blockchain-based technology is the best solution for the problem that needs solving, and if the answer to this question is yes, then (*b*) whether there is a cost-benefit analysis that skews the answer in favor of a blockchain implementation. Since we are still in the early stages of this technology, there is not a lot of information available about the true cost of developing solutions and the challenges that will be encountered. For that same reason, there are also not too many experts in the field who have the experience and ability to develop these technologies for libraries. That all being said, the goals of this chapter were to spur on the imagination and provide thought starters in the hope that the ideas will inspire and maybe lead to the eventual development of blockchain-based applications for libraries.

Notes

1. A public blockchain for all libraries not to be confused with a blockchain only for public libraries.
2. Artory home page, last accessed September 8, 2019, https://www.artory.com; "The Barney A. Ebsworth Collection Sale—A Landmark for the American Art Market," Christie's, last accessed September 8, 2019, https://www.christies.com/features/Barney-Ebsworth-Collection-results-9552-3.aspx.
3. American Library Association, *Privacy: An Interpretation of the Library Bill of Rights* (Chicago: American Library Association, adopted June 19, 2002; amended July 1, 2014, and June 24, 2019), www.ala.org/advocacy/intfreedom/librarybill/interpretations/privacy; American Library Association, *Library Bill of Rights* (Chicago: American Library Association, adopted June 19, 1939; amended October 14, 1944, June 18, 1948, February 2, 1961, June 27, 1967, January 23, 1980, and January 20, 2019), www.ala.org/advocacy/intfreedom/librarybill.
4. News Provenance Project, "About," accessed September 7, 2019, https://www.newsprovenanceproject.com/About.

Chapter 4

Barriers and Challenges to Blockchain Implementation in Libraries

As mentioned in the introduction, the majority of blockchain-based applications so far have been in the cryptocurrency space. As a result, it remains to be seen how blockchain will be implemented in business and industry. There certainly seems to be widespread interest in the technology as many of the benefits continue to become clearer. However, turning over existing processes to blockchain has not and will not be without challenges. Below is a brief discussion about several questions related to various barriers and challenges libraries face with respect to implementing blockchain-based systems.

Technological Know-How

While blockchain will be touted as the panacea for many library problems, the reality is that blockchain and its implementation are complex. Knowledge about implementation and applied use cases is still very limited. The challenge that arises then is which of the organizations working with libraries will be the first to pursue this opportunity and start creating blockchain-based applications for libraries? Will libraries be able to develop blockchain applications individually, or will we come together via our consortia or through partnerships? Where will the technology leadership come from to introduce libraries to blockchain?

Choosing the Right Blockchain

As has been illustrated in the case studies mentioned in chapter 3, blockchain is not a simple, one-size-fits-all solution. Just as there are many vendors for library systems, there are many blockchain suppliers and platforms. National and international vendors will come offering products and support. Some libraries will have competent technology and development teams that can build the infrastructure from scratch. We may also find that some of our consortia will start participating. Once the right blockchain platform has been chosen, do we want to develop our own apps on the platform, subscribe, or buy existing products? Do we have enough information about whether we want to implement private or public blockchains?

The answers to these questions will present themselves in due time. Before long, the first proofs of concept will be developed, and hopefully the developers will share them with our community. Once they do, we will be able to test the applications, and many of the questions above and below will be answered.

Cost of Implementation

Any new technology carries many inherent costs. Naturally, the direct dollar costs must be considered in the selection of a product, in the development or customization, in the deployment, and so on. However, indirect costs will also be incurred in having to train our library employees on new systems. Will the switchover be immediate and complete or gradual? Perhaps costs will be incurred in having to carry two systems for some duration. And, ultimately, the question is how do these costs compare to the benefits derived from this system? Will the benefits outweigh the costs? And, if so, over what period of time?

Cost of Maintenance and Development

Once libraries have taken the plunge and committed themselves to a blockchain-based application, the costs of maintenance and development must be considered. They may not differ significantly from the costs we incur in maintaining our current systems; however, library salaries are typically not competitive with the salaries offered by industry. As a result, there may be challenges in attracting and retaining the talent to work on our blockchain-based solutions in libraries.

Chapter 5

Ethical and Other Considerations

As libraries explore the feasibility of implementing blockchain-based applications, a number of issues and questions arise that are beyond the scope of the technological implementation. These issues are ones that decision makers and those working in and with libraries will have to reconcile in order to effectively move forward and take advantage of this transformative technology.

Who Owns the Blockchain?

The blockchain that underlies any application has to be developed and set up. However, who or which entity is responsible for setting up the blockchain? Once the blockchain is set up, the question arises about who "owns" it. The argument could be made that nobody owns a public blockchain and it lives in the cloud as a distributed technology. However, every blockchain has to have a supervising authority that determines rules and approves modifications. In the case of Ethereum, a not-for-profit foundation with voting members has been set up. How would that process adapt to libraries? Who would own the blockchain? Who would oversee it?

Who Owns the Data?

Blockchain is a data-based application where stored data is encoded in the blocks. The nature of blockchain is such that if the blockchain is actively in use, then the amount of data stored rapidly grows. The question arises, then, of who owns the data in the blockchain? Is it the owner of the blockchain? Is it the libraries contributing data to the blockchain? In a consumer application, do the users of the blockchain own their own data? Or, perhaps, the notion of ownership of data in a blockchain is misplaced. Perhaps the blockchain is a public good? If the blockchain is private, does that change who owns the data? Are all parts of the data "ownable"? Perhaps the blockchain is owned or coordinated by one entity (such as a not-for-profit organization or consortium) while the data in the blocks is owned by its producers. And, if the data can be owned, what does that ownership actually mean and authorize its owners to accomplish?

How Secure Is the Blockchain?

While blockchain is a technology based on cryptographic principles designed to ensure security, the system itself is not infallible. In a public blockchain, the blocks that have been added to the blockchain are immutable, and the consensus requirement of 51 percent provides a layer of security. Could libraries ensure the same level of participation? How would we incentivize the participation of distributed computing nodes to verify or mine the blockchain? In a private blockchain or open-source blockchain (e.g., Hyperledger), how do we audit the integrity of the data? Could the owner of the blockchain modify the record at any time? Could the owner use authorization for root access to subvert the integrity of the blockchain? In cryptocurrency applications, great efforts have been made to ensure the blockchain's privacy and security, and we should make an effort to learn from those efforts if we pursue blockchain within our organizations.

Unintended Consequences?

Of course, this section is dipping into the great unknown. As we explore blockchain and its ability to transform libraries, we will no doubt learn about its many benefits and encounter challenges we could not have anticipated. How do we work with patrons who have lost their private key? What will we find out about the energy consumption required? What will we find out about the technological requirements? How about the costs associated with developing and maintaining the blockchain? These are the unknowns of new technology, and it stands to reason that every "unhackable" technology poses an invitation for hackers to find ways to defeat it. As computing power increases, the race will continue to develop better cryptographic standards to stay a step ahead of hackers.

Legislation and Regulation

At this point, it remains unclear what the future holds for blockchain regulation. The case for cryptocurrencies has been made, and they have been established as functional, decentralized currency. However, one of the most significant critiques of cryptocurrencies has come from legislators. They are concerned that cryptocurrencies have enabled avoidance of regulation and taxation that apply to regulated currencies. This has led regulators to review ways that cryptocurrency can be regulated and taxed. This, of course, is counter to the entire decentralized nature of blockchain. However, as a result of this increased scrutiny into blockchain technologies, libraries may possibly face similar concerns around issues of data and user privacy. The General Data Protection Regulation (GDPR), introduced by the European Union in 2018, is an example of the complexity that is introduced when one jurisdiction (the EU in this case) imposes rules that have far-ranging effects. The rules were introduced by the EU, but any organizations conducting business in or with the EU have to align their data practices with these rules, thus effectively changing the global landscape regarding data and security. The rules were designed to empower individuals to have more control over the data collected about them on the internet. Individuals can instruct a company to remove any of the digital records it has on them. The enactment of these GDPR rules also has an important impact on blockchain. If the blockchain is indeed immutable, then the request of an individual could not be honored, which could lead to significant fines against the organization holding the data. However, it remains to be seen how this scenario will play out. It is conceivable that as blockchain evolves, more regulation will come into place that will further impact how the technology will be implemented.

General Data Protection Regulation
https://eugdpr.org

This chapter illustrates just how many unanswered questions there are with regard to blockchain and libraries—questions that extend beyond the technical and really touch on the ethics of blockchain. Considering these questions is of the utmost importance, especially in the information profession. Our motives and ethics in libraries are such that these are paramount issues we ought to resolve or at least be aware of. One by one, the questions will be answered as libraries walk down the path of blockchain development and implementation. At the same time, as some questions are answered, new ones will reveal themselves. My goal in introducing these questions is to raise awareness and hopefully create a dialogue or motivate an investigation into some of them.

Chapter 6

Conclusion

Change in the blockchain space is happening quickly and often. At this point, it is unclear which projects will prevail and which ones will fail. Platforms are competing with each other to gain market share. Derivatives of blockchain technology are springing up daily and are looking to gain traction in both public and private domains. Facebook recently proposed its own blockchain-based cryptocurrency.[1] The reach of this cryptocurrency would be dominant as it would instantly reach Facebook's 2+ billion users. An open-source, Linux-based private blockchain initiative called Hyperledger is also gaining momentum and has significant corporate support. Ethereum is an open-source platform that enables blockchain development. The Enterprise Ethereum Alliance has signed up many significant commercial partners. Many consulting firms, banks, and other industries are reviewing how they might incorporate and leverage blockchain in their business processes. The cynic in me thinks that blockchain is a trend right now, attracting a lot of interest, and many, if not most, projects will never even see the light of day. However, the optimist in me believes that too many smart and motivated people are working on this technology for it not to provide valuable applications in a range of arenas. Thus, I expect to find blockchain-based applications, or at the very least attempts to establish blockchain, in libraries within the next few years. Perhaps one of our suggested use cases will become a reality. However, more than likely, it will be something we have not thought of yet—and that is just fine. Either way, these are exciting times to be involved in these conversations as this technology has the potential to end up influencing and perhaps even transforming the work of libraries. There is no easy answer as to whether blockchain will be the right solution for solving the complex issues we face in libraries. There are many factors to be considered, but in libraries we are always eager to learn and experiment. We sometimes do it locally and sometimes systemwide or consortially. So only time will tell whether blockchain ends up being a fad or a relevant technology. However, if we do not consider the potential applications for this technology in libraries and educate ourselves, we risk falling behind—let's not do that. Let us boldly commit to blockchain and learn about how libraries can benefit from this incredible technology.

Hyperledger
https://www.hyperledger.org

Ethereum
https://www.ethereum.org

Enterprise Ethereum Alliance
https://entethalliance.org

Note

1. Libra, "An Introduction to Libra," white paper, last revised July 23, 2019, https://libra.org/en-US/white-paper.

Notes

Notes

Notes

Library Technology REPORTS

Upcoming Issues	
January 56:1	**Digital Rights Management and Books** by Mirela Roncevic
February/ March 56:2	**Digital Disruption** by Bohyun Kim
April 56:3	**Voice Assistants in Libraries** by Win Shih